WINDS

ETON AND RUNNYMEDE

A Brief History

10th century
Windlesora has a Saxon settlement and a royal palace.

1154–89
Henry II rebuilds part of the castle in stone. A park is enclosed in the forest.

1215
King John sets his seal to the Magna Carta at Runnymede.

1440
Henry VI founds Eton College.

1475
Edward IV begins St George's Chapel.

1509
Henry VIII moves his court to Windsor. The town prospers.

c.1070
William the Conqueror builds a castle on a chalk hill.

1110
Henry I transfers his court to Windsor Castle. The town begins to grow.

c.1230
Henry III develops the castle. A bridge links Windsor and Eton.

1348
Edward III reconstructs the royal apartments and founds the Order of the Garter.

1547
Henry VIII is buried in St George's Chapel beside Jane Seymour.

1597
Shakespeare's 'The Merry Wives of Windsor' is performed for Elizabeth I.

1642–9
During the Civil War Charles I is imprisoned at the castle.

1660–85
Charles II restores the castle and chapel, and creates the Long Walk.

The beautiful riverside town of Windsor owes its beginnings to William the Conqueror, who built his earth and timber stronghold on a chalk hill by the Thames some 900 years ago. Outside the castle walls the first houses were built, and as the castle increased in importance, so did the town. Since the earliest days, the fortunes of the town have risen and fallen with the monarchy's interest in the castle. Many sovereigns made Windsor Castle their principal residence and the trade this generated brought prosperity to the town, not least because of the ambitious building schemes that were carried out. But at times the town fell into great poverty and squalor.

In 1917 the Royal Family adopted 'Windsor' as their family name, and it is in Windsor that Her Majesty The Queen feels most at home, in a palace built by many generations of her ancestors, surrounded by extensive parkland, stunning gardens and a majestic river.

1689
Sir Christopher Wren completes the Guildhall.

1711
Queen Anne establishes a race meeting at Ascot.
1776
George III makes Windsor his home and is a familiar sight in the streets.

1820–30
George IV transforms the neglected castle into a splendid palace, increasing the height of the Round Tower.

1837
Queen Victoria resides at Windsor.
1849–51
The Great Western and South-Western Railways arrive.

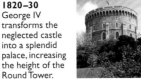

1901
Queen Victoria is buried next to Prince Albert at Frogmore.
1917
George V adopts 'Windsor' as the name of the Royal Family.

1939–45
Princesses Elizabeth and Margaret live at Windsor Castle during the Second World War.
1970
Windsor Bridge is pedestrianized.

1992
Fire destroys part of the Upper Ward of the castle.
1997
Repairs to the state apartments are completed.

1999
Prince Edward and Sophie Rhys-Jones are married in St George's Chapel.

Windsor Castle

A royal palace in the Saxon settlement of Windlesora (meaning a riverbank with a windlass, or hoisting machine) was acquired for William the Conqueror within a year of his coronation. Just two miles north of this palace stood a steep chalk hill overlooking the Thames – the highway of southern England – beside a vast area of superb hunting forest, and it was here that the king built an earth and timber stronghold as one in a ring of defences around London. When Henry I transferred his court from the palace to the castle, he took the name Windsor with it. The Saxon town became Old Windsor, and the new town of Windsor grew up beneath the castle walls.

Today's castle is the product of centuries of rebuilding, extending and refurbishment by England's kings and queens. Its wealth of history and treasures will delight and fascinate all who visit it.

QUADRANGLE

Overlooked by the equestrian statue of Charles II, the Quadrangle comes alive with colour and pageantry during State Visits.

ROUND TOWER

Actually an irregular oval in shape, the Round Tower was built by Henry II in 1170 to replace the Conqueror's wooden structure, and heightened by 30ft for George IV in the 1820s. It stands on the original mound and is surrounded by a dry moat, now the beautifully kept garden of the Governor of the Castle.

VISITING THE CASTLE

Normally open to visitors every day of the year except Good Friday, Garter Day and Royal Ascot Week in June, Christmas Day and Boxing Day, the castle's opening arrangements are subject to change because it is an official residence of The Queen. Her Majesty's presence is marked by the flying of the Royal Standard from the Round Tower. Allow at least two hours for your visit.

NORTH TERRACE

A wonderful panoramic view of the Thames Valley and Eton College (▷ 24–25) can be enjoyed from the North Terrace.

Horseshoe Cloister

King Henry VIII Gate

KING HENRY VIII GATE

Built in 1511 and decorated with Henry VIII's symbols, this gate has holes in its vault, through which boiling oil could be poured on unwelcome visitors.

NORMAN GATE

Between the twin towers of the Norman Gate, built by Edward III in the 14th century, is an arch that holds a portcullis.

HORSESHOE CLOISTER

Situated to the west of St George's Chapel, this attractive row of brick and timbered houses was built in 1480 to provide good lodgings for the Lay Clerks (men of the choir) who still live there today.

CASTLE GUARD

Windsor Castle's guard is usually provided by one of the Foot Guard regiments. One of the highlights of a visit to Windsor is the colourful Changing of the Guard ceremony (▷ 11).

Changing of the Guard

State Apartments

The State Apartments, used by The Queen for ceremonial, state and official occasions, are elaborately decorated with a wealth of magnificent treasures. Superb painted ceilings complement glorious tapestries, fine woodwork, splendid French and English furniture and important works of art, many of which were saved from the devastating fire of 1992.

King's Dining Room

FIRE OF 1992

On the morning of 20 November, 1992 – The Queen and the Duke of Edinburgh's 45th wedding anniversary – a blaze started in the Private Chapel in the north-east corner of the castle and quickly spread, devastating five major and several lesser state rooms. Providentially, these rooms had been emptied due to a rewiring project but, nonetheless, for each of the 15 hours that the fire lasted, £2.4 million damage was done. As the inferno was brought under control by courageous firefighters, castle staff and members of the public formed human chains to rescue priceless treasures from adjoining rooms.

REPAIR AND RESTORATION

While some rooms were restored to their original forms, those that had been completely destroyed were redesigned. Architects were invited to submit designs for the new St George's Hall, and from the variety of styles that emerged, the Royal Household chose the splendid modern Gothic design by the Sidell Gibson Partnership. The area that had been occupied by the Private Chapel was transformed into the beautiful octagonal Lantern Lobby. In November 1997, after five years of skilled work and craftsmanship, the restoration was complete, and The Queen and the Duke of Edinburgh held a ball at the castle to celebrate their Golden Wedding anniversary.

St George's Hall

Queen Mary's Dolls' House

This exquisite dolls' house, given as a gift in 1924 to Queen Mary, wife of George V, is a masterpiece in miniature that fascinates and delights all who see it. Designed by Sir Edwin Lutyens as an accurate record of an early 20th-century English palace, it is a work of impeccable quality, with decorations and contents made in the finest materials by leading English craftspeople and artists of the day. Built on a scale of 1 to 12, it is accurate to the very last detail, with silk curtains, jade ornaments, 'Chippendale' furniture, marble floors, and the most up-to-date facilities, including working lifts, lights and hot and cold running water.

Queen Mary's Dolls' House: Queen's Bedroom

Miniature piano and books from Queen Mary's Dolls' House

St George's Chapel

The historic chapel of St George in the Lower Ward of the castle is one of England's most beautiful religious buildings. Built in fine Perpendicular style, it was started in 1475 by Edward IV as the Chapel of the Order of the Garter, and completed 50 years later by Henry VIII. Lavishly embellished with a magnificent fan vaulting and intricate carving and ironwork, it is the burial place of ten monarchs.

FAN VAULTING

The remarkable stone vaulted roof of the chapel is richly decorated with roof bosses showing the arms and devices of the Sovereign and Knights of the Garter as well as other symbols.

CHOIR AND CHANCEL

The banners of the Knights of the Garter hang above the magnificent carved woodwork of the choir, started by William Berkeley in 1478 and extended in the 1780s. Behind the stalls can be seen some 670 stall plates of previous knights, including that of Sir Winston Churchill. A stone in the central aisle marks the burial vault of Henry VIII.

ALBERT MEMORIAL CHAPEL

The interior of this 15th-century chapel was decorated in high-Victorian style for Queen Victoria, in remembrance of her beloved husband, Prince Albert, who died in 1861.

St George's Chapel

ST GEORGE

Known to have been a Christian soldier martyred at the beginning of the 4th century in Palestine, St George was adopted as the Patron Saint of England and the Order of the Garter after the Crusades. The most famous legend of St George tells the story of a pagan town in Libya which was plagued by a dragon. The townspeople, having attempted to placate the beast with offerings of sheep and members of their community, decided to present the ultimate gift – their princess. As the dragon prepared to devour the beautiful maiden, the gallant George galloped onto the scene and slew the dragon before setting about converting the community to Christianity. His feast day is celebrated on 23 April.

Edward III

THE ORDER OF THE GARTER

Britain's highest order of chivalry, the Order of the Garter, was founded in 1348 by Edward III. A popular story behind the Order is that its motto, '*Honi soit qui mal y pense*' ('Shame on him who thinks evil of it'), were the words uttered by the king in response to shocked courtiers when he retrieved a lady's slipped garter from the floor. The colourful Garter Day pageant takes place each June. The Queen and 24 Knights, dressed in robes of the garter – including a blue garter buckled below the left knee – process from the Upper Ward to the royal chapel for a service of thanksgiving.

Order of the Garter Procession

Windsor Town

This delightful town, whose fortunes have been so affected by the castle, bears the souvenirs of many eras. The charming network of cobbled streets behind the Guildhall, known as 'Guildhall Island', developed on the medieval market place that stood outside the castle walls. It now contains many 17th-century buildings. Park Street is lined with elegant Georgian houses and the imposing Royal Station is a fine example of Victorian civic architecture.

Peascod Street in about 1908

STATUE OF QUEEN VICTORIA

At the centre of the town stands the solemn bronze statue of Queen Victoria, erected on the site of the medieval market cross in 1887 to mark the 50th year of her reign.

TOWN AND CROWN EXHIBITION

Situated above the Royal Windsor Information Centre in the High Street, this compact but comprehensive exhibition gives an insight into the history of the town using audio-visual displays.

Queen Victoria statue

PEASCOD STREET

Now Windsor's main shopping street, Peascod (pronounced 'pesscot') Street originally led to a medieval field known as Peas Croft. The street has an entrance feature which shows two medieval dancing scenes. Further along on the left, a bull's head, set high in the wall, is evidence of the slaughterhouse and butcher's shop that once stood on the site. At No. 86–7 stands a handsome timber-framed building that was restored in 1976.

GUILDHALL

Legend has it that when Sir Christopher Wren had completed the Guildhall in 1689, the council insisted that the slender outer columns alone were not sufficiently strong to support the Council Chamber above. Wren added four internal columns, defiantly leaving them a little short of the ceiling to prove that his design was sound.

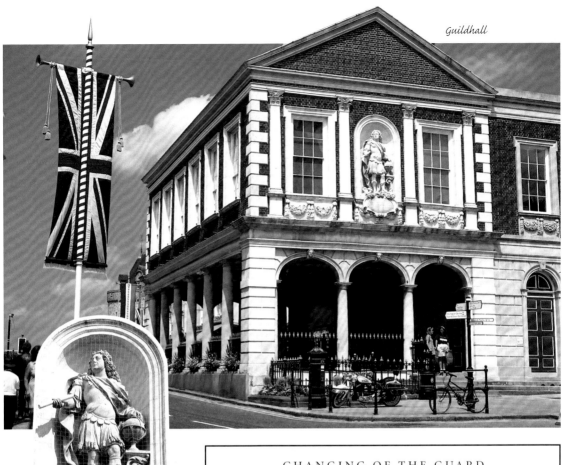

CHANGING OF THE GUARD

With the exception of Sundays, the Changing of the Guard takes place in Windsor Castle mostly every day from late spring to mid-summer, and on alternate days at other times of year. The marching band leaves Victoria Barracks in Sheet Street at 10.45 a.m., and marches swiftly up the High Street to arrive in the castle at about 11.00. At 11.30 the old guard marches back to the barracks. Visitors can enter the castle before 11.00 to watch the Changing of the Guard, or take up a place in the High Street or Castle Hill and see the band arriving in their striking, colourful uniforms. Following the band back to the barracks is an invigorating experience.

POST BOXES

Beside the Guildhall is a Victorian post box in green, gold and black livery. Further down the high street is a blue post box which commemorates the first-ever airmail, from Hendon to Windsor in 1911.

Windsor Town

MARKET CROSS HOUSE

Next to the Guildhall (▷ 10) stands the leaning, timber-framed Market Cross House, built as a butcher's shop in the butchers' shambles in 1718. Its crooked appearance is thought to be due to structural alterations made in the 18th century.

QUEEN CHARLOTTE STREET

Recorded in 'The Guinness Book of Records' as the shortest street in England, Queen Charlotte Street is just 52ft long.

> ENGINE HOUSE
> MDCCCIII
> DANIEL SMITH
> CHARLES JARMAN } CHURCH
> JOSEPH SHARMAN } WARDENS
>
> The Keys are with the Church Wardens & the Sexton

CHURCH LANE

The Engine House, with its rather quaint notice over the entrance, is where Windsor's fire engine was kept during the early 19th century. The building next door dates from 1423, and is one of the oldest houses in the town.

CHURCH STREET

On the outside wall of the 1525 Old King's Head is a copy of the warrant issued to execute King Charles I in 1648, and among the signatories is Oliver Cromwell. The 1640 house next door, with its unusual timber-framed wings, is reputedly the former home of Charles II's favourite mistress, Nell Gwynn. It is said to be haunted by two ghosts, one of whom was killed in a fire and brings the smell of burning with him.

Church Street

WINDSOR PARISH CHURCH

The church of St John the Baptist, built in 1822, stands on the site of a 12th-century church of the same name, and contains many memorials preserved from the Norman church. The church's greatest treasure is 'The Last Supper', a magnificent painting of unknown origin, given by George III following alterations to the royal chapel. Windsor Parish Church is a brass-rubbing centre, containing brasses from all over Britain and Europe.

SHAKESPEARE

William Shakespeare stayed in Windsor in 1597 while writing 'The Merry Wives of Windsor', to be performed for Queen Elizabeth in the castle. He found background material for his play by talking to people in the streets, and completed the work within 14 days.

BACHELORS' ACRE

An alleyway almost opposite the parish church leads through a car park to Bachelors' Acre. Now a small public park with a children's play area, it was formerly Windsor's town green, and often the site of public celebrations and fairs. At the north-east corner of the park is Western Cottage, built in 1702, where the Reverend S. J. Stone wrote the hymn 'The Church's One Foundation'.

Windsor Parish Church

Windsor Town

THAMES STREET

Metal inserts still to be seen in the gutter of Thames Street prevented horse-drawn carriages from rolling down the hill.

ROYAL STATION

The Great Western Railway arrived in Windsor in 1849, and 48 years later a magnificent station and façade were built for the Diamond Jubilee celebrations of Queen Victoria. Today, these imposing Victorian buildings are combined with exciting designer shops in a superb retail development.

Royal station

BOOTS PASSAGE

Named after the famous chemist shop which once stood next to it, Boots Passage displays a tiled aerial view of the castle, based on a 1663 engraving by Wenceslaus Hollar. Set above the entrance is a bust of the popular monarch Edward VII.

Castle from Alexandra Gardens

ALEXANDRA GARDENS

Laid out in 1903, this park is popular with young people and incorporates a roller rink and cycle hire centre.

THEATRE ROYAL

The Theatre Royal was established in Thames Street in 1815 but most recently rebuilt in 1911 following a fire. Originally situated in Peascod Street (▷ 10) in 1775, Windsor's theatre has been patronized by members of the Royal Family through the centuries. It offers a full and varied programme, including classic drama, new musicals and traditional pantomime.

ROYAL WINDSOR MAZE

A brick path maze which, inspired by the castle, features chess pieces, is laid out in The Goswells between Thames Street and Goswell Road. The challenge is to reach the round tower at the centre of the maze by walking in one direction, and by passing through each chess piece only once.

WREN'S HOUSE

Now an hotel, this late 17th-century pedimented house by Windsor Bridge is believed to have been built by Sir Christopher Wren as his family home.

WINDSOR BRIDGE

Windsor and Eton were first linked in the 13th century by a wooden bridge. A pontage, or toll, was charged to those who passed over or under the bridge, to pay for its upkeep. The present cast-iron bridge was completed in 1824 and was closed to motor traffic in 1970 when it was discovered to have structural problems.

Horses

The Great Park was one of Windsor's main attractions for keen royal hunters, and it was Queen Anne's enthusiasm for horses that inspired her to have a racecourse constructed at Ascot. Now many equestrian events are held in Windsor each year, including polo matches, racing and the Royal Windsor Horse Show.

EQUESTRIAN STATUES

The Castle Quadrangle's equestrian statue of Charles II dressed as Caesar was erected in 1680. A huge statue known as the Copper Horse (▷ 18) stands at the end of the Long Walk.

Charles II in the Castle Quadrangle

WINDSOR RACECOURSE

Set in beautiful countryside on the banks of the Thames, Windsor Racecourse is just a ten-minute trip by river. Its restaurants, cafés and fast food bars open every race day.

HORSE-DRAWN CARRIAGE RIDES

Surely the most elegant way to tour Windsor is in a horse-drawn carriage. The ride lasts for 30 minutes or an hour, and takes you from Thames Street down the tranquil Long Walk.

RACING AT ASCOT

Evening and daytime races are held throughout the year at Ascot, though the highlight of the season is Royal Ascot week (▷ 30), held each June.

ROYAL WINDSOR HORSE SHOW

Windsor's hugely popular annual horse show is held each May in the Home Park.

Royal Windsor Horse Show: King's Troop Royal Horse Artillery

POLO MATCHES

Polo matches are played on most weekends through the summer at Smith's Lawn in the Great Park (▷ 18–19). The Cartier International match at the end of July is the highlight of the season.

Queen Victoria's grandchildren, 1890

Windsor Great Park

The 4,800-acre area of Windsor Great Park is the remains of a huge and ancient forest, where Saxon and Norman kings hunted the plentiful deer and wild boar. Poachers were commonplace, and in the early 12th century the Great Park was formed when part of the forest was enclosed for the safe keeping of the deer. Hunting has continued to be popular with kings and queens residing at Windsor, most notably James I, who would wallow in the blood of his kill, and Queen Anne, a passionate huntress who would hurtle around the park in a single-seated hunting chariot.

COPPER HORSE

This huge equestrian statue of George III depicts the king as a Roman Emperor, riding on a charger without stirrups, wearing a toga. It was erected at the request of his son, George IV.

LONG WALK

The beautiful three-mile avenue that runs from the castle to the Copper Horse on Snow Hill was laid out for Charles II in *c*.1680. It is along this route that the royal party travels to the Ascot Racecourse during Royal Ascot week (▷ 30). The Long Walk is reached via Park Street.

SAVILL GARDEN

Created in 1932 by the park's deputy ranger, Sir Eric Savill, this woodland garden is considered one of the finest of its type. Its alpine meadows, secret glades and colourful flower gardens create a peaceful refuge, with wonderful displays of colour all year round.

FROGMORE HOUSE

Situated in the Home Park amidst fine and tranquil gardens, Frogmore House dates from *c*.1680. Queen Victoria's mother, the Duchess of Kent, spent much of the last 20 years of her life at Frogmore, and was buried in an elegant mausoleum in the grounds. The house became the favourite retreat of Queen Victoria after the death of her husband, Prince Albert, and they are both buried in a grand mausoleum which they built for themselves. Frogmore House is open on a limited number of days in May and August each year, when visitors may explore the finely decorated rooms and the picturesque gardens.

Savill Garden

VIRGINIA WATER

This famous lake was created by the Duke of Cumberland, son of George II, and is said to be named after Elizabeth I, the virgin queen. On the northern bank of the lake are the Valley Gardens, stocked with colourful azaleas, magnolias and rhododendrons. The totem pole that stands at the northernmost tip of the lake was erected in 1958 to mark the centenary of British Columbia, and is 100ft tall.

River Thames

The broad River Thames flows majestically around the historic town of Windsor, attracting many visitors to its waters and banks. Walkers and cyclists on the Thames Path enjoy the activity on the water, as pleasure boats of all kinds drift by and swans glide peacefully to and fro.

ETON COLLEGE BOATHOUSES

At these boathouses the Eton College sculls and skiffs are built, maintained and stored. On afternoons and evenings during the rowing season, from April until July, Etonian 'wetbobs' can be seen practising on the river.

MUTE SWANS

The river at Windsor is graced by hundreds of mute swans, Britain's commonest breed. All the swans on the Thames are owned by Her Majesty The Queen and the Vintners' and Dyers' Livery Companies, and are allocated at an ancient ceremony each July called Swan Upping, in which the cygnets are weighed, ringed and recorded.

Castle from the Thames

THE FOURTH OF JUNE

Eton College's tradition of celebrating George III's birthday arose from the great affection that the Etonians of that day felt for their king, who would often stop outside the school and chat with the boys between 'divs', or lessons. For those who choose to be 'drybobs' the highlight of the Fourth of June is a cricket match, while for 'wetbobs' it is the Procession of Boats on the Thames, in which the oarsmen, wearing flower-laden boaters, get to their feet in the boats and shake the flowers into the water.

BOAT TRIPS

Relaxing river cruises of various lengths offer visitors a different perspective on the area, with stunning views of the castle and Eton College. Rowing boats and motor boats may be hired from a station on Barry Avenue, and cruisers may be boarded from the promenade, east and west of Windsor Bridge.

Eton High Street

Across the river from Windsor lies the quiet town of Eton, once a Saxon settlement surrounded by marshland, and, since 1440, home to the most famous school in the world. Until the closing of Windsor Bridge in 1970, Eton High Street was the main route from Windsor to Slough, thronging with buses and lorries. Now relieved of heavy traffic, the High Street manifests an old-fashioned charm and, lined with specialist, art and antique shops, is a collector's heaven.

PUBLIC ART

A series of stainless steel bollards welcomes visitors to Eton on Windsor Bridge. Made by jeweller Wendy Ramshaw, each bollard has a different decorative top, and a special 'tower' bollard incorporates an optical lens which offers visitors a surprising view of Eton High Street and Windsor Castle.

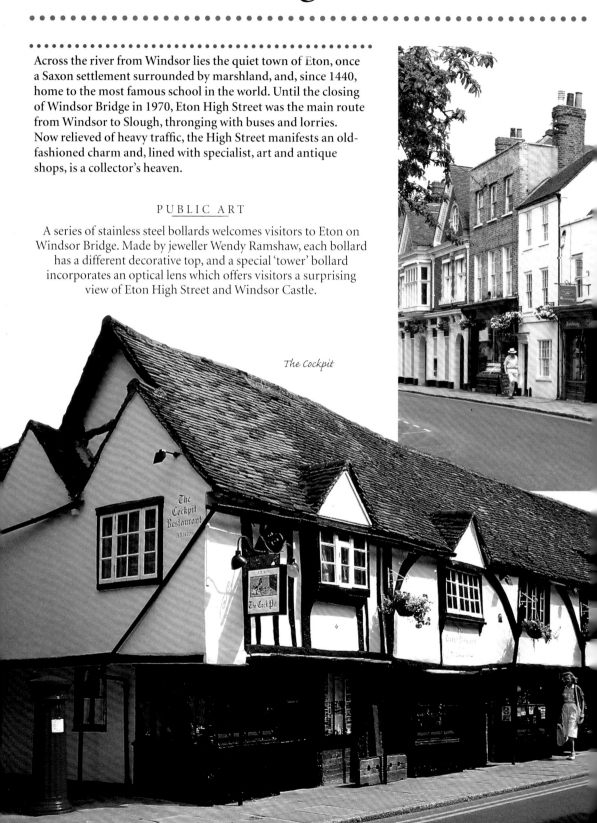

The Cockpit

Eton High Street

ASQUITHS TEDDY BEAR SHOP

Eton sports kit

THE COCKPIT

This charming building, dating from 1420, has the remains of what some believe to be an old cock-fighting pit at the rear, which may be viewed on request. In front of the building is an ancient set of stocks, and beside it is a rare Victorian post box.

THE BROCAS

Owned by Eton College, this large expanse of riverside meadow is a pleasant place for a stroll or a picnic. Each August a funfair is held here.

LITTLE TREATS IN WINDSOR AND ETON

• A stroll along the Long Walk (▷ 18), or beside the River Thames (▷ 20–21).

• Watching the guards as they march towards the castle for the Changing of the Guard (▷ 11).

• Choral services at St George's Chapel (▷ 8–9) and Eton College Chapel (▷ 25).

• Window-shopping under the glass vaulted roof of the Royal Station concourse (▷ 14).

• Browsing amongst the fascinating shops of Eton High Street (▷ 22–23).

• A real English cream tea in one of the tea rooms around the Guildhall (▷ 10).

• A leisurely boat trip on the Thames (▷ 20–21).

......Cat Out of the Bag

01753-854800

Gifts
Cat Lovers

Eton College

In 1440, at the age of 18, Henry VI founded 'The King's College of Our Lady of Eton beside Windsor', lavishing it with generous funds and manifold privileges. The 70 poor scholars for whom Henry provided continued their education at King's College, Cambridge, which he founded the following year. Today Eton's world-famous public school still offers scholarships to 70 students, and takes an additional 1,200 fee-paying pupils, or 'Oppidans'. Guided tours of the college are available (▷ 27), and visitors can discover more of its fascinating history in the Museum of Eton Life.

ETON'S EARLY DAYS

Conditions were harsh for Eton's early scholars, with all 70 boys sleeping in the Long Chamber, several to a bed, and washing at an outdoor pump in the nearby cloisters. The scholars were fed two meals a day except on Friday, which was a day of fasting. They were permitted to speak only Latin, and were allowed home just once a year, in the summer.

MEMBERS OF POP

In the early 19th century a newly formed debating society met in a local lollypop shop, and quickly became known as 'Pop'. Now the school's prefects, 'Poppers', are recognised by their colourful waistcoats, spongebag trousers and braid-edged tailcoats.

chapel wall paintings

SCHOOL YARD

School Yard is surrounded by the college's oldest buildings: Lower School, the College Chapel, Lupton's Tower and Upper School. At the centre of the yard stands a bronze statue of the founder in Garter robes.

LOWER SCHOOL

Eton's only classroom for 200 years, Lower School was in use by 1443 and is one of the oldest classrooms in the world. Its wooden desks, benches and pillars are carved with the names of generations of Etonians.

COLLEGE CHAPEL

When he was deposed in 1461, Henry VI's plans for a cathedral-sized church were scuppered and building was brought to a halt before a nave had been added. It was not until 1479 that Bishop Wayneflete, a former provost of Eton, roofed the choir in wood and added an antechapel to the west end.

The magnificent Perpendicular Gothic chapel contains extraordinarily fine Flemish-style wall paintings, completed in 1487. These were covered in whitewash by the college barber at the bidding of Reformers in 1560 and eventually restored in 1923. The chapel roof's mock fan vault, made of composition stone suspended from steel trusses, was completed in 1959.

Runnymede

Just three miles south-east of Windsor, on the banks of the winding River Thames, is the famous meadow of Runnymede, where King John set his seal to the Magna Carta in 1215.

MAGNA CARTA

Seal of King John

King John's baronial opponents drew up the Magna Carta, a set of agreements which would prevent future monarchs from abusing their power by raising taxes without first consulting the barons, or by imprisoning people without a fair trial. The king was persuaded to sign this 'Great Charter' but had no intention of keeping to it.

JOHN F. KENNEDY MEMORIAL

A simple but touching memorial to John F. Kennedy, erected in 1965, stands in an acre of ground given to the USA by The Queen in memory of the assassinated president.

THIS ACRE OF ENGLISH GROUND WAS GIVEN TO THE UNITED STATES OF AMERICA BY THE PEOPLE OF BRITAIN IN MEMORY OF JOHN F. KENNEDY BORN 29 MAY 1917 PRESIDENT OF THE UNITED STATES 1961-63 DIED BY AN ASSASSIN'S HAND 22 NOVEMBER 1963 LET EVERY NATION KNOW WHETHER IT WISHES US WELL OR ILL THAT WE SHALL PAY ANY PRICE BEAR ANY BURDEN MEET ANY HARDSHIP SUPPORT ANY FRIEND OR OPPOSE ANY FOE IN ORDER TO ASSURE THE SURVIVAL AND SUCCESS OF LIBERTY

Runnymede

TRIPS AND TOURS IN WINDSOR AND ETON

For up-to-date information on the seasonal availability of all trips and tours, phone the Royal Windsor Information Centre on 01753 743900.

Boat trips: (▷ 21) Thames cruisers operate from two points on the riverside path near Windsor Bridge.

Walking Tours of Windsor and Eton, led by an expert Blue Badge Guide, are available for groups, and can be booked in advance by phoning 01494 873697.

Guided Tours of Eton College (▷ 24–25) are available from March to October, but parties of ten or more must book in advance by phoning 01753 671177.

Open-top buses giving a guided tour of Windsor and Eton can be boarded at Castle Hill, or at any of their route stops.

Horse-drawn Carriage Rides along the Long Walk (▷ 18) can be taken from the taxi rank in Thames Street.

A special bus service to Legoland (▷ 28–29) operates from Windsor town centre.

COMMONWEALTH AIR FORCES MEMORIAL

High on the hill, in beautifully tended grounds, stands the Commonwealth Air Forces Memorial, a poignant tribute to 'the men and women of the airforces of the British Commonwealth and Empire who lost their lives serving from bases in the United Kingdom and North-West Europe in the Second World War and who have no known grave'. The names of 20,455 airmen and women are recorded on the stone panels of the colonnaded courtyard.

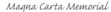

Magna Carta Memorial

MAGNA CARTA MEMORIAL

On the wooded hillside overlooking the lush water meadows stands the memorial erected in 1957 by the American Bar Association commemorating the Magna Carta, on which the American Constitution is based.

TO COMMEMORATE MAGNA CARTA SYMBOL OF FREEDOM UNDER LAW

Legoland® Windsor

Carefully laid out in a large area of wooded parkland, Legoland promises an action-packed day of fun to all its visitors. The seven themed areas offer exciting rides, activities and attractions particularly suited to children aged 2–12, and parents or grandparents can join in all the fun while appreciating Legoland's meticulous attention to safety and convenience.

Miniland   *L-School*

MINILAND

Famous cities and sights of Europe, buzzing with computer-controlled ships, trains and buses, are recreated in the fascinating Miniland. Using around 20 million Lego® bricks, it took a team of 100 model makers almost three years to complete Miniland, but would have taken one person 67 years!

Dragon Ride

Pirate Falls

FUN RIDES

Legoland's rides range from the Duplo® train and the Dragon's Apprentice for the youngest visitors to the thrilling Dragon Ride roller coaster. Those prepared to get wet might brave the Pirate Falls and the Extreme Team Challenge.

VISITING LEGOLAND

Situated just two miles out of town, Legoland can be reached by a special shuttle bus service from Windsor's railway stations, or by car. For information on opening times and for bookings phone 0990 040404.

EDUCATIONAL PLAY

The Imagination Centre offers creative and challenging play activities, including technology sessions to introduce children to the world of robotics using Lego Mindstorms 'intelligent' RCX bricks.

ENTERTAINMENT

Contemporary circus acts, spectacular stunt shows, traditional fairytales and fables and interactive musical fun are all performed live at various venues in the park, while hilarious entertainers roam the grounds.

TRAFFIC

While youngsters develop their driving skills at L-School, older children receive a road safety lesson at Driving School, then take their driving test in an electric car on a real road network, negotiating traffic lights, pedestrian crossings and roundabouts. Participants in the Boating School navigate a course of buoys and bubbling rapids in a powered boat, while intrepid adventurers can test their aptitude for heights at the Balloon School.

Out of Town Visits

Visitors wishing to explore beyond Windsor and Eton will find several delightful features in the Great Park (▷18–19). Upriver from Windsor, many attractive villages nestle on the banks of the Thames, while the surrounding countryside of downs, woods, heaths and wetland entices the walker.

DORNEY COURT

Built in *c.*1440 and lived in by the present family for over 450 years, Dorney Court is one of the finest late medieval manor houses in England. Open on selected days during May, July and August, the house contains family portraits and fine English furniture collected by the family through the generations. Dorney is situated three miles north-west of Windsor.

ROYAL ASCOT

It was in 1711 that Queen Anne first inaugurated a race meeting at Ascot, and today Royal Ascot week is considered one of the most important events of the social and sporting calendar. This is partly due to the keen interest shown by the Royal Family, members of whom arrive in royal procession from Windsor prior to each day's races. Royal Ascot is enjoyed not only for its top-quality racing and garden party atmosphere, but also for the opportunity it presents to dress up. Gentlemen in top hats and tails escort ladies flaunting the very latest designer outfits, always complemented by a flamboyant hat.

Dorney Court

SHIRE HORSE CENTRE

Magnificent prize-winning horses can be seen at the Courage Shire Horse Centre at Maidenhead, eight miles west of Windsor. Previously employed in pulling the brewers' heavy carts, the shire horses are now used for showing and promotional work. Attractions include a farrier's workshop and cart rides.

ODDS FARM PARK

Many of Britain's rarest and most interesting farm animals are bred at this delightful farm park, ten miles north-west of Windsor at Wooburn Common, High Wycombe. Created with children in mind, it provides lots of opportunities for them to observe the animals closely and safely.

STANLEY SPENCER GALLERY

The pretty village of Cookham, nine miles north-west of Windsor, was the birthplace of the leading 20th-century visionary artist Stanley Spencer. His love of this village, where he spent most of his life, strongly influenced his work, much of which can be seen at the Stanley Spencer Gallery.

DISCOVERY OUTPOST

Discovery Outpost

Situated ten miles south-west of Windsor, Bracknell's hands-on science centre has over 70 interactive exhibits. It is surrounded by 2,600 acres of Crown Estate woodland known as the Look Out Discovery Park, which has walks, an orienteering course, mountain bike hire and an adventure playground.

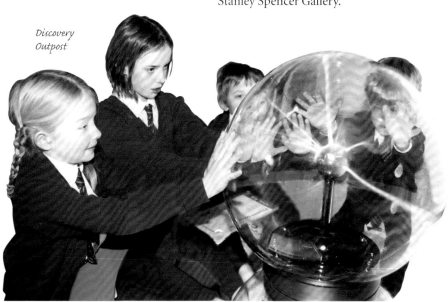

Town Plan

 ROYAL WINDSOR
INFORMATION CENTRE
24 High Street
Windsor SL4 1LH
telephone: 01753 743900
fax: 01753 743904

SHOPMOBILITY
For the loan of manual or powered
wheelchairs and electric scooters
for those with limited mobility,
telephone: 01753 622330

WHAT'S ON

Full information on these annual events and festivals is available from
the Royal Windsor Information Centre.

May	Royal Windsor Horse Show in Home Park
	Frogmore House and Gardens open days (▷ 18)
	Royal Windsor International Horse Trials
	in the Great Park
June	Queen's Cup Polo at Smith's Lawn
	Garter Ceremony (▷ 9)
	Royal Ascot Race Meeting (▷ 30)
	Royal Windsor Triathlon
Jun–Aug	Horse racing at Windsor Racecourse every
	Monday evening
July	Royal Windsor Dog Show in Home Park
	Royal Windsor Flower Show
	Swan Upping on the Thames (▷ 20)
	Cartier International Polo at Smith's Lawn
August	Funfair on The Brocas, Eton
	Knowl Hill Steam Rally
	Plant fair at Savill Garden
September	Windsor Festival
	Classic Car Show and Auto Jumble at Ascot Racecourse
October	Laser, Light and Fireworks Show at Legoland®

CHORAL SERVICES

The famous choirs of St George's Chapel (▷ 8–9) and of Eton
College Chapel (▷ 25) sing regular services in term-time, at which
visitors are very welcome.

Choral evensong is sung by St George's Chapel Choir every weekday
in term-time except Wednesdays, and on Sundays. Visitors who wish
to attend a service must gather at Henry VIII Gate (▷ 5) at 5.00 p.m.

The choir of Eton College Chapel sings regular services throughout
the week and on Sundays in term-time, details of which are posted
on the chapel's High Street door, or can be obtained by phoning the
Precentor's secretary on 01753 671169.

During the summer holidays members of the public may attend
services and concerts sung by members of the Eton Choral
Courses. For details phone 01753 671171.

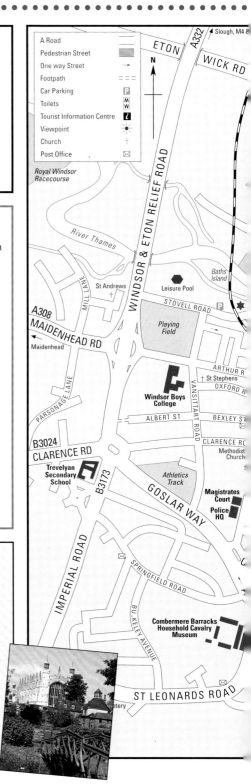